➤ DEDICAT

CW01431829

To: _____

From: _____

"I wish for you a life of wealth, health
and happiness; a life in which you give to
yourself the gift of patience, the virtue of reason,
the value of knowledge, and the influence
of faith in your own ability to dream about and
to achieve worthy rewards."
— *Jim Rohn*

SPECIAL SALES
SUCCESS books are available at special discounts for bulk purchase
for sales promotions and premiums. Special editions, including
personalized covers, excerpts of existing books, and corporate
imprints, can be created in large quantities for special needs. For more
information, contact Special Markets, SUCCESS, sales@success.com.

SUCCESS

THE **JIM ROHN** GUIDE TO **TIME MANAGEMENT**

➤ JIM ROHN ◄

For more than 40 years, Jim Rohn honed his craft like a skilled artist, helping people all over the world sculpt life strategies that expanded their imagination of what is possible. Jim set the standard for those who seek to teach and inspire others. He possessed the unique ability to bring extraordinary insights to ordinary principles and events. Those who had the privilege of hearing him speak can attest to the elegance and common sense in his material. It is no coincidence, then, that he is widely regarded as one of the most influential thinkers of our time and a national treasure. Jim authored numerous books and audio and video programs, and he helped motivate and shape an entire generation of personal development trainers and hundreds of executives from America's top corporations.

For additional information or to shop for Jim Rohn's best-selling books, CDs, DVDs and more, go to www.JimRohn.com.

➤ A NOTE ON THIS GUIDE ◄

The text of this pocket-size guide is based on transcripts of Jim Rohn's most popular lectures and writings on the subject of time management. His original words have been transcribed, edited, rearranged and slightly modified in some instances for greater clarity.

As you read, you may recognize a familiar pace to the text. It is our hope that Jim's easy conversational tone and speaking style come across in your reading of each and every page. Though some of Jim's references may be out of date, his life philosophies and success principles transcend the years and are as relevant today as they were when he first expressed them.

The intent of this guide is to provide a concise, easy-to-read treatment of the subject matter that can be read in a short sitting of 15 to 20 minutes. Highlight your favorite parts and keep it close for easy reference again and again. Share it with friends, family, associates, clients and anyone you feel would benefit from the timeless wisdom of a true legend.

See page 48 for information on other booklets in the Jim Rohn Guide series.

THE **JIM ROHN**
GUIDE TO
TIME
MANAGEMENT

Let's talk about time management. I've got several approaches to the management of time. Here's the first approach. Ignore the subject. That's valid. A guy says, "Hey, I've been late all my life and it doesn't look like all this time management's going to work for me. I just ignore it." That's wonderful. And I say that really to make this point: Remember, be a student, not a follower. Design your own personal life. I'm very happy for people to take notes at my seminars. But I'm also just as happy if someone says, "Hey, this is not for me." Tear up all these notes and throw them away. That's just as valid for me. Remember, be no one's disciple. Chart your own course, make what you do the product of your own conclusion. This is valid—ignore the subject.

Here's another approach to time management. Step down to something easier. If you're getting hassled by the management of time, you might want to change course. What I'm saying here is be your own person. You don't have to be a model of someone else. You don't have to do it like anybody else. Do it like yourself. Buy what you want to buy, listen to what you want to listen to, make changes if you want to make changes, and don't make changes if that's what you want. It's your life. And don't let anybody persuade you any different.

➤ THE DIGNITY OF CHOICE ◄

Success is not a stereotype. Success is not a Ferrari. Success is not an automobile. It's not a house. It's not a place. It's not money in the bank. It's not a million dollars. That's not success. Success is the continual unfolding of the design of your own life and pulling it off. That's what success is. Being successful in whatever you want to do that makes sense to you, for you and your family. Take on responsibilities or refuse them, it's all up to you. We've been given the power of choice.

Every life form except human beings operates by instinct in the genetic code. It has no multiple choice. Only humans have multiple choice. In the winter the goose flies south. Why? Because he's a goose. He can't fly north. He couldn't fly west. If you said to the goose it'd be better to go west this year, he ignores that advice. He keeps on flying south. Why? He has no alternative. He has no other way. He is only driven, as all life forms are driven, by instinct in the genetic code.

Except human beings. Now why not human beings? Because we've been given the dignity of choice. We're not like a robot. We're not stuck like a tree, using up all the nourishment and, with nothing left, you die because you can't change locations. Not true. Humans can go north, south, east, west. Humans can change and do anything they want to do. We've been given the dignity.

But here's what's interesting about all life forms except humans: Every life form except humans strives to the max of its potential. How tall will a tree grow? As tall as it possibly can. You've never heard of a tree growing half as high as it could. No, that is impossible. A tree grows as high as it can, drives down every root it can, produces every leaf it can, extends itself as far as it possibly can. Every life form extends to the max, except human beings. Now why not human beings? Because we're not robots. We've been given the dignity of choice.

➤ DO IT ALL OR DON'T ◄

Be part of or all of what you have the potential to be. You've got the choice. Do a little to make yourself comfortable and forget the rest, or do it all. There's nobody here to dictate you've got to do it all. That's nonsense. You've got to be rich because we live in a rich country. That's nonsense. You don't have to be rich. You don't have to do it all. You can do a little, do some, do some more. Take advice, but don't take orders. Take information, take training, take teaching, but don't take orders from anyone that tells you how you need to live and what you need to own and what you need to do. Somebody says, "Well, you need to be successful." That's a personal choice, being successful. What we teach is the possibilities, and everybody chooses. Take a little, take a lot, do some, do nothing, or ignore the subject. This is why I put this in here. You've got to learn to do that.

Abraham Lincoln said, "As I would not be a slave, so I would not be a master." Excellent philosophy. A guy says, "Hey, I'm soon cashing it in and I'm heading for the mountains. I'm going to live in a little cabin, live off the land and feed the squirrels." If he goes and does that, guess what—he's a smashing success. Why? He's doing what he designed to do and pulled it off. You can't say, "No, no, that's not successful." That is the epitome of success—giving a design to your life and pulling it off to make progress in the direction that satisfies you. If it doesn't satisfy you, make alternatives and change. If you get some better ideas, sure you may follow someone's suggestions and ideas but not orders.

> **DESIGN YOUR OWN LIFE** <

Design your own life like you want it. Now if you take on some responsibilities, you've got to consider those. Yes, you can ignore your responsibilities, but you won't feel good about that. Here's what the old prophet said: "Some things that taste good now in the mouth turn bitter later in the belly." So you don't want to sacrifice.

We all must suffer one of two pains: the pain of discipline or the pain of regret. What we suggest to everybody is to consider the disciplines because disciplines weigh ounces; regrets weigh tons. You don't want to substitute a discipline for a regret. In our opinion that would be a poor choice. Now you can do it, but some things are poor tradeoffs. The old prophet said, "What if you gain the whole world but it costs you your soul?" Would that be worth it? With a bit of intelligence, we say no, that doesn't seem worth it even if you've got the whole world if you traded your soul. That experience would be so bitter and so awful and so devastating, it wouldn't be worth it.

What if you got some gain by greed instead of legitimate ambition? I'm telling you, it might taste good up front, but it's going to turn bitter in the belly. And a bit of that advice saves some people from devastation. Say, "Well, you're right. I'd better think twice about that." So we must confront all laws. Spiritual laws, agricultural laws, basic laws, fundamental laws. We must confront all of those. But you still now can design your own life. A little or a lot. Go east, north, south.

➤ **WEIGH THE COST** ◄

So, time management might be to step down to something easier that doesn't stress you with the constraints of time. A guy works for a company, he says, "Oh, I've got to own one of these." He finds out he's now got to work 24 hours a day, all around the clock. And he's got to worry about all these people. The guy says, "The heck with this. I'm going back where I used to be. I played golf three times a week and made three times as much money as a salesperson. The heck with this running a company."

That's the deal. Don't put yourself in the straitjacket of something that's not to your choosing and not to your liking. Now if you really want the prize, to become a multimillionaire and run a company, fine. Then you've got to pay the price. But hey, it's strictly up to you. There're no requirements here. Where is it written? There is no law. The key is to try to design your life. Yes, you might try something and say, "This costs me too much. I'm away from my family, I'm gone." So this is valid.

A little girl said to her mommy, "Daddy never plays with me. He comes home and he's got this briefcase and he disappears and works on his papers and he tells me to go to bed." Mom tried to explain and said, "Look, your father loves you very much, but he's so busy at work that he can't get everything done and he has to bring it home." The girl said, "Why don't they put him in a slower group?" Not a bad idea. If you haven't got time for your kids, you should consider a slower group. It's not the money. It's not the success. You've got to make sure everything works. Not something at the expense of everything. At the expense of everything turns out to be too costly.

➤ **BALANCING ACT** ◄

Life at its best and most fulfilled, I think, is a balancing act to make everything work. A mother's got the challenge, a father's got the challenge, and all of this in balance, even the tug of war trying to make it work as husband and wife. A guy's a baseball player and he gets four or five million dollars a year, and his talent takes him away 185 games, whatever the number of games are that they play. That's a pretty tough one to do. Gone most of the time. Should he go where his talent leads or should he work at the bank from 9 to 5? It's a challenge to try to fit, compromise, make it work, make all systems work so you don't sacrifice everything for something. It's all a dilemma.

If you've got partners, now it's the combination of working it out. But let me tell you what, it can be worked out. Here's what happens if you ignore it. It just gets worse. You've just got to confront and say, "Let us work it out so that we bless our life with all of the systems that furnish us with a good life." Guess what? It never ends, this trying to balance your life with everything.

So, in the management of time, step down to something easier, rearrange your program, pick up someone else's advice—not orders, but advice that says, "Hey, I went for the money instead, and it cost me too much." Here's the real time management: Make yourself more valuable. Get more from yourself so that you become much more accomplished in an hour that used to take a week. That is the easiest of time management, to make yourself more valuable.

So now, let me quickly give you the rundown here, some key pieces to time management.

➤ **MAJOR VS. MINOR** ◄

Here's a key phrase: Either you run the day or it runs you. Getting in charge, mastering the situation, this is the big challenge. I remember some companies I started years ago. I'd start the company and I'm running the company. First thing you know, the company's running me. Along about that second year, I say, "Hold it, hold it. I used to be in charge and now I'm out of control. I use to have it on the run, now it's got me on the run." And the same is true whether it's a company or an enterprise or whether it's the day. The key is you've just got to take charge and say, "I'm going to start getting a handle and taking charge of my day and not let it get out of control." Because it's so easy to be persuaded and distracted by things that use up time, and then the first thing you know, it's all out of control.

It's not that difficult to get something started and you run it for a while and after a while it starts running you. That's part of the challenge. I told my staff one day that giving birth to a tiger is one thing, but learning how to ride it is something else. Sometimes you start it and then it turns around and starts giving you all kinds of trouble.

Here's the key we've all learned, and maybe we just need to be reminded. It's not the hours you put in; it's what you put in the hours that count. A guy comes in at night exhausted, he falls into the chair and says, "I've been going, going, going." Doing what? Don't mistake movement for achievement. Busy, busy, busy, that may not be the deal. It's the doing what that's the deal. Some people are busy all day long doing figure eights. They're not making much forward progress. They keep coming back around where they started.

Here are some time management essentials.
Learn to set goals so that you have some
priorities. Then, constantly review your priorities
to make sure it's what you really want.

Learn to separate majors and minors. Here's
something that requires minor time. Here's
something that requires major time. Here's
what we teach in sales: the most important
time in a salesperson's career is time in the
presence of the prospect. That's the most
important time. Time in the presence of
the prospect—that's called major time.

Here's minor time—on the way to the prospect.
Making plans to see the prospect, that's called
minor time. In the presence of the prospect, that's
major time. Keeping files on the prospect, that's

minor time. Thinking about prospects and how it's going to go in the future, that's called minor time. Here's major time—in the presence of.... So you've just got to arrange your career so that most often you're in the presence of. Not on the way to, not keeping books on, not thinking about, not making records for, but in the presence of. Now the minor things are important, but they're minor things. Make sure you don't spend major time on minor things.

➤ **CONCENTRATION** ◄

Next key to time management is concentration.
You zero in if you concentrate. Many times it
takes a lot less time when you concentrate. If
you get distracted, it takes a whole day because
of the distraction. But if you concentrate, it
could take an hour instead of a day. It could
take a few minutes instead of a half a day.

I read this little article in *Reader's Digest*. It said,
"Wherever you are, be there." Concentrate there.
I used to try to design my day in the shower. I'm
not even awake yet and I'm trying to write a letter.
What I finally learned to do is enjoy the shower.
Don't start the day till you get to the work. On
the way, enjoy the way. At breakfast, enjoy the
breakfast. Some guys in business, they're already
at the office at the breakfast table. The key is to

be at breakfast with your family at the breakfast table. There's plenty of time to do the business when you get to the office. You can't compose the next letter eating your cornflakes. Now you've got to concentrate on your family. Wherever you are, be there. Concentrate there. That's a key.

Next, learn to say no. It is so easy, especially now in a social society to just be pulled everywhere with social obligations. Do you say yes, yes, yes, yes? Then you find yourself so overloaded on your calendar that it eats up all the time. So learn to say no politely. It's easier to say, "I don't think so, but if that changes I'll call," than to say, "Oh, yes," and then try to figure out ways to make the call and not to make it. One of my colleagues says, "Don't let your mouth overload your back." Because it's easy to just oblige, wanting to be nice, wanting to be pleasant, wanting to please. But you get pulled in too many directions by saying yes too easy too frequently and finding yourself in a box.

➤ WHEN YOU WORK, WORK ◄

Now here's a big one on time management. When you work, work. When you play, play. Don't mix the two. Here's the big one. Don't play at work. Here's why: work is too serious. Guess what economics is? Serious business. Economics is a serious subject because you're trading part of your life being economically sustained and providing protection for you and your family for generations to come. This is a serious deal. The one place you don't horse around or fool around is at work. Somewhere else, yes. At work, no.

Just establish that reputation that you don't fool around at work. Yes, a little pleasantry and, yes, a little story to relieve the tension, but you just don't play around at work. You've got to consider work like the farmer in the spring. He can't play around. He's only got a short season. And you can't go distract him and have him play around. This isn't playtime. This is work time trying to plant a straight row, get everything right in the short season we've got. This is no time to joke around. So develop that reputation not just for other people but for yourself, for your own self-esteem, that says when you work, you work. So don't play at work.

Now here's the rest of it: Don't work at play. I used to be at the office and I'd say, "I've got to take my family to the beach. It's been so long. What does my family think? We've got to get to the beach." So I'm thinking beach while I'm at work. Now I get to the beach with my family, thinking I should be at the office. What am I doing here at the beach? Now my family's bent out of shape because, yes, I'm at the beach, but I'm also at the office. So here's what I learned to do: At the office be at the office, and at the beach be at the beach with your family. Don't mix the two. When you work, work. When you play, play.

➤ ANALYZE YOURSELF ◄

Next on time management—analyze how you are and see if you can at least be covered. If you're not good at something, then get somebody to take care of it instead of delaying all of the time doing it yourself. Either compensate for it or change. If you've tried to balance your checkbook for about a year or two, that's long enough. Just put the money on some accountant's desk and say, "Look, take care of this for me." It doesn't have to be very much, just so it's taken care of. Either you do it or you can let somebody cover for you and get it done so that you can concentrate on more essential, more important things.

If you're a morning person, that's probably the time to get the best of your work done. Now some people they're not awake at 11:00 yet, so we call these night people. At midnight they're still flying. But at 11:00 they're not quite awake. I'm now more of a morning person. I used to be the night person, now I'm more of a morning person. Way back years ago I used to say, "If God meant you to see the sunrise, he'd have made it later in the day." But now I love the mornings. The mornings are fresh and clean. The unique thing about starting the day in the morning, you haven't messed it up yet. The whole day is fresh and clean. Guess what you have in the morning—a clean page. "Let's see, I don't want to mess this one up. Let me make some plans here to make this an extraordinarily good day." That morning time is very unique if you become a morning person. But whatever you are, just analyze how you are. Whatever you're not good at, see if you can get it covered.

➤ BEWARE OF THE PHONE ◄

Way back in those early days I remember, before I learned to just ignore the phone or unplug it, and back then you couldn't even unplug it, you had to just let it ring. I used to have friends over and the phone would ring and I'd say, "Just let it ring. We're having a conversation." My friends couldn't stand the phone to ring and not answer it. So they'd go answer my phone. They'd say, "It's for you." I'd say, "Yeah, I suppose it is."

But here's the key—with all the new stuff now, here's what you've got to do at home—you've got to shut everything off and have dinner with your family. You just shut everything off. Now they've got it where the messages will be taken and everything will be taken, but you've just got to say this time, we shut out the world. It doesn't matter if the president calls. It doesn't matter who calls. They've got to wait for at least an hour till I'm finished with my family. Your family will take great delight in you shutting out the world. Just shut everything off for a while. There's plenty of time to get back to it. You say, "Well, what if some emergency is happening?" It'll have to wait.

➤ **READ THE BOOKS** ◄

Here's another key on time management. Read the books. If you need some specific help, there's a book for it. There have been many books written on time management. Take their advice, but still make your own plans. Become more aware and alert to all the new technology now available that can save your time. Stay in touch.

Here's another big-time management principle, especially if you're working with people. Learn to ask questions before you launch into some tirade or launch into some personal seminar. Sometimes you talk for a half hour, ask a couple of questions and find out you just wasted the previous half hour.

Here's what you should've been talking about. So here's the key, ask questions up front. "John isn't making sales." I'll say, "Hey, call John in and I'll tear him a new page." Well, before you do that you'd better ask, why isn't he making sales? Someone says, "Well, he's not getting up early and getting out in the marketplace." He says, "Get him in here, and I'll teach him some get-up-early stuff." Well, before we do that we'd better ask one more question, "Why isn't he up early and out in the marketplace?" So we call John in and say, "Hey, John, it's got to be something personal. You're not up early. You're not out in the marketplace." He says, "Yes, I never thought anyone would ask." You just ask, "What is it?" Rather than launching into something, save the time, ask the questions up front.

Now here's one more tip on asking questions. Sometimes you don't find the problem until you go two, three questions deep. Because most people don't just blurt out what's wrong first question. Most problems are two, three questions deep. Right away, somebody wants to know if they're going to tell their problem to somebody who doesn't really care, so you've got to establish some connection. Then somebody's willing to disclose. Kids are like that. Say, "How's it going?" They say, "Okay." That okay doesn't sound right. That doesn't ring right. Something tells you it isn't okay. So you've got to ask the next gentle question and then the third gentle question, and finally they say, "Yeah, here's the real problem." Learn to ask questions up front. That's the key.

➤ **THINK ON PAPER** ◀

Learn to think on paper. You solve problems on paper. Let me give you some ways to think on paper. Number one: keep a journal. I used to have three journals. One for business, one for personal, one for a book I was writing. That was too complicated. Then I tried colors of ink. Blue means this, red means this. I got rid of that. Now I just fill one up, and then fill another one up and fill another one up. Include personal ideas, a little bit of diary. And that's all it is. Here's what a journal is: a collection of your notes and a bit of a diary and what's going on in your life. It's just a way to capture it in a bound volume.

I used to keep notes on pieces of paper, torn off corners, backs of old envelopes, restaurant placemats thrown in a drawer. Guess what? They didn't serve me well. It was okay for the time, but now trying to find something or going through it, it's not enticing. So then I learned finally to start putting it in a journal. A bound volume. It's a little more enticing on a winter day to just sit down and go back through your journal.

Sometimes when I'm off somewhere and I don't have my journal, I'll jot some things down and when I get back to my journal I'll put them in there, and throw the paper away. Just little ideas like that. You just have to decide whether you need a big one or a small one or a light one or an easy one. But just go. Just start keeping more records of ideas that come your way, whether it's a recipe or a colossal business idea or the schedule for the next few ball games that are coming up. It doesn't matter what. Just load stuff in there and then load up another one and load up another one. You will be proud someday that you kept these journals.

➤ PROJECTS BOOK ◄

Next, another pretty good idea: a projects book. Whatever project you're working on, get a three-ring binder and keep little notes on that project and how it's going. When you finish the project, you file it somewhere. But as long as that project is active and going, keep that projects book.

Now I know you can put it all in the computer and you can study that. But for me, I like the regular three-ring binder for the projects I'm working to give a little running account of how it's going.

If you're working with a person, you record that person's name and just keep a little running account of how it's going between you and the person. If you're in sales, you've got some salespeople in there to keep track of. Give them each a page. Give them each a partition in your projects book. When you're about to speak to them, do a little review of what you talked about last time. Now you're better prepared to talk to them this time. It becomes a briefing book.

When the president gets ready to make a trip to another country, his staff briefs him. They tell him, "When you were there before, here's what you talked about. When you were there before, here are the promises you made. When you were there before, here's who you met and here's who they are and here's what you said." And he briefs himself on all of this so that when he goes again, he says, "I remember last time when I was here."

These briefing books provide an interchange of both project and person. A little running account of how it's going, what this person did last month, what they're doing this month. Even with your children, you can track how they are progressing. They started a little project. How's that project going? "Well, I helped them do this, and I helped them do this. Is it time for me to lend them a little more assistance?" Just keep a little record of the people and the projects until it's finally finished and then you file it away.

Don't forget a scheduler or day timer. You've got to keep track of where you're supposed to go and who you're supposed to meet. You know, just load all that stuff in there instead of trying to keep it in your head. I jump in the limo to head for the airport. The driver says, "What airline?" And I say, "I'll have to look" because I don't store it in my head. Maybe I'm kind of freaky like that. Rather than keep all this stuff loaded in my head, I just find a convenient place to put it where it's all available. Keep your head open for bigger projects than what airline.

➤ GAME PLAN

Develop a game plan where you schedule all the things you've got to do, laying out six months or a year or longer. A game plan is pretty simple because it has a list of all your projects that you want to accomplish, and then you put them on the calendar.

I found out if your project book is in one place and your calendar is in another place, it gets to be a little confusing. So you have a game plan for a project and schedule how it's going to work for the next six months, year or more. You say, "Well, I'm going to do some advertising." That's the project. And, "I'm going to do some here, some here, some here, and some here."

It can work for whatever program you've got going, whatever you want to accomplish. For your health program, you say, "I'm going to go to the gym here. I'm going to run this marathon here. I'm going to do this. I'm going to do this. This is my health program." You see the advantage there is when the project list and the game plan calendar are side-by-side instead of one being in one place and another in another place.

You've got to put your family on there too. The family wants to know where they fit in the game plan. So you start talking, and they say, "No, show me." Wouldn't kids go for that? "Show me where I am on the game plan." You say, "Well, you're right here and you're right here and you're right here, and you're right here." They say, "That's all I need to know." Don't kids want to be on your game plan? And it's better visual than conversation.

Now, let's say you've got a project in your company and you have to go to your family now because you want to use family time. You make a deal. You say, "Look, I've got to knock you out of this because I've got a work project. It's going to mean so much for the business and it's going to mean so much for the family. We'll be able to do so many more things, but I've got to borrow this time." Now you have the payback. "If you let me borrow this time, we'll pay it back here and we'll do this, this and this." They'll say, "Well, that's okay if you'll do this, this and this." I mean, once kids have got you, they're going to go for the max. But wouldn't kids be more reassured if they knew they were on your game plan, even though it has to change at times? Even though some emergencies or whatever rearrange the deal? "As long as I'm on the plan." We simply call this a game plan.

➤ A FINAL THOUGHT ◄

It's an obvious—yet often overlooked—truth: rich people have 24 hours a day and poor people have 24 hours a day.

The difference between the rich and the poor is in the management of that time. Successful people often work harder and longer than most, but they almost always work smarter.

If we get more from ourselves, if we can make an hour as valuable as 10 hours used to be, we can get as much done in a day as we used to get done in a week. Imagine the potential compounding effect of working smarter.

By practicing the few simple disciplines discussed here every day, you can use time like the rich—with focus and effectiveness.

THE JIM ROHN GUIDE SERIES

The timeless wisdom of Jim Rohn in concise, easy-to-read guides. Perfect for sharing with friends, family, business associates, clients and prospects.

TIME MANAGEMENT
PERSONAL DEVELOPMENT
LEADERSHIP
GOAL SETTING
COMMUNICATION

Quantity discounts available
JimRohn.com or
store.SUCCESS.com